BROADWATER SCHOOL

Charities
Poverty
Famine
Oxfam

OXFAM

By Kirsty Holmes

WORLD
CHARITIES

BookLife
PUBLISHING

©2018
BookLife Publishing
King's Lynn
Norfolk PE30 4LS

A catalogue record for this
book is available from the
British Library.

ISBN: 978-1-78637-313-7

Written by:
Kirsty Holmes

Edited by:
Madeline Tyler

Designed by:
Dan Scase

WORLD CHARITIES

CONTENTS

Words that look like **THIS** are explained in the glossary on page 31.

CHARITY & GIVING

Some people give money to charity.

WHAT IS 'CHARITY'?

Every person and animal on planet Earth is part of a GLOBAL COMMUNITY. We all need similar things to survive and grow. Every person needs food to eat, fresh water to drink and somewhere safe to live. But, even though we all need the same things, we don't all have the same things. Some people and animals have access to more RESOURCES or are better protected from danger than others.

Donations

Some people give their time to help others.

For example, in some countries there may not be enough food for people to eat, or there may be wars or natural disasters which have taken away people's homes. Animals are also in danger all over the world, often because of human activity.

VOLUNTEER

Some people help animals in danger, like these tigers.

Many people see these problems and feel a strong need to make it better. They help by giving time, money or other resources, such as food, to those in need. This type of giving is called charity.

WHAT IS A CHARITY?

When a group of people get together and form an organisation to help people, animals or other good causes, we call that organisation a charity. Charities can be huge, **INTERNATIONAL** organisations with thousands of people working for them, or they can be small groups working for a local good cause. People **DONATE** their time and money to charities, and in turn, the charities organise these resources to help people in the best way possible.

Some charities are like big companies, organising thousands of people and millions of pounds.

Small local charities, like hospices or animal sanctuaries, rely on people's donations.

People can do silly things to raise money for charity!

KEY WORDS ABOUT CHARITIES

- **Donation** — a gift of time, money or goods to a charity
- **Donor** — a person or company who makes a donation
- **Volunteer** — a person who works for a charity but isn't paid
- **Fundraising** — collecting money for a charity
- **Awareness** — making sure people know about a charity or issue
- **Campaign** — work in an organised way towards a goal
- **Activist** — person who campaigns and raises awareness on a topic

OXFAM

THE OXFAM CHARTER

Together we can achieve a fairer world without poverty.

Oxfam is an international **CONFEDERATION** of 20 organisations working together with partners and local **COMMUNITIES** in more than 90 countries.

One person in three in the world lives in poverty. Oxfam is determined to change that by mobilising the power of people against poverty.

"Around the globe, Oxfam works to find practical, innovative ways for people to lift themselves out of poverty and thrive. We save lives and help rebuild **LIVELIHOODS** when crisis strikes. And we campaign so that the voices of the poor influence the local and global decisions that affect them.

In all we do, Oxfam works with partner organisations and alongside vulnerable women and men to end the injustices that cause poverty..."

> A charity's values tell you what they stand for, who they want to help, and why.

> Poverty is when people don't have enough money to live on. If someone is in poverty, they cannot pay for food, clothing or somewhere to live.

Find out more about Oxfam's mission at https://www.oxfam.org/en/about

HOW OXFAM BEGAN

WE WON'T LIVE WITH POVERTY

The Oxford Committee for Famine Relief was formed in Oxford, England in 1942. The first meetings tackled how the group could help with a FAMINE that was occurring in Greece at the time, caused by the Second World War. The charity quickly grew, and by 1960 it was already a major international operation, under the name Oxfam.

In 1949, Oxfam's Joe Mitty opened a shop in Oxford, selling donated clothing to raise money. The idea of selling on anything people were willing to give became very popular, and Oxfam now has a chain of hundreds of shops up and down the UK.

Oxfam is a charity and organisation working to end poverty. They began by providing food to people who were starving, but have grown into a huge international organisation, helping where it's needed and fighting to end poverty once and for all.

This plaque on the wall tells people how special this shop is.

The first permanent OXFAM shop began trading here in December 1947

Oxford is famous for its universities.

The First Oxfam Shop, in Broad Street, Oxford

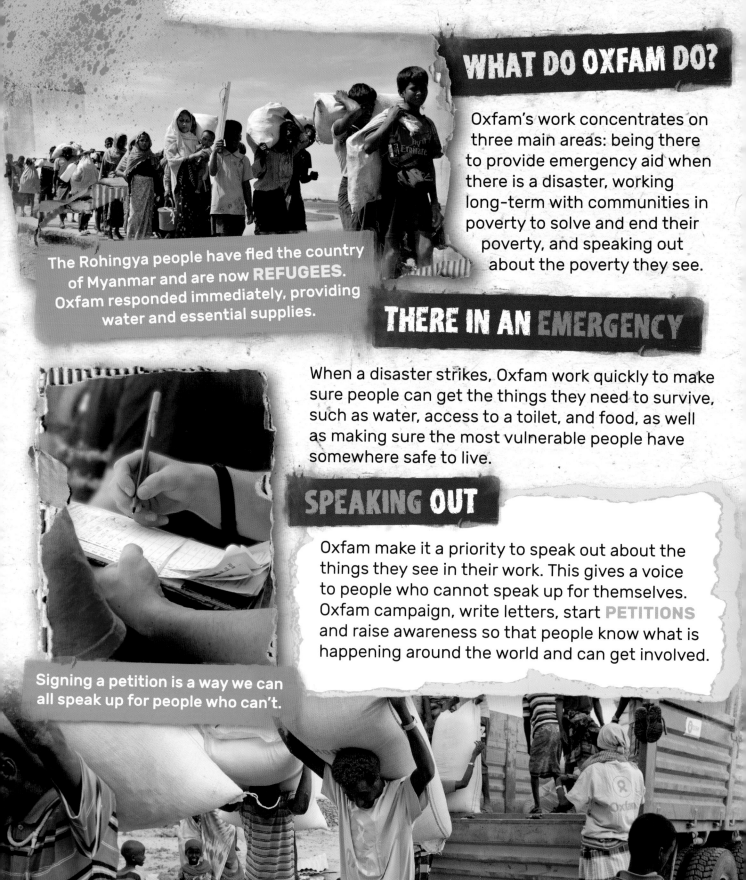

WHAT DO OXFAM DO?

Oxfam's work concentrates on three main areas: being there to provide emergency aid when there is a disaster, working long-term with communities in poverty to solve and end their poverty, and speaking out about the poverty they see.

The Rohingya people have fled the country of Myanmar and are now REFUGEES. Oxfam responded immediately, providing water and essential supplies.

THERE IN AN EMERGENCY

When a disaster strikes, Oxfam work quickly to make sure people can get the things they need to survive, such as water, access to a toilet, and food, as well as making sure the most vulnerable people have somewhere safe to live.

SPEAKING OUT

Oxfam make it a priority to speak out about the things they see in their work. This gives a voice to people who cannot speak up for themselves. Oxfam campaign, write letters, start PETITIONS and raise awareness so that people know what is happening around the world and can get involved.

Signing a petition is a way we can all speak up for people who can't.

THERE FOR THE LONG HAUL

Oxfam works to raise awareness and educate people, teaching us that, in a world so rich with resources, no one should have to live in poverty. They also work to help people improve their situations by giving loans to help them start businesses, or improve their existing ones. Oxfam also aim to speak out, helping people understand **INEQUALITY** so that we can learn to live in a way that respects everyone's rights. People who work for Oxfam also help with campaigning, raising money and supporting those who look after people living in poverty.

After an emergency, it is important that charities, like Oxfam, work with the affected communities in the long term too. Oxfam works to help make communities more able to come back strong after a disaster, and to be better prepared in the future.

This is wahida. wahida had to leave her home in Iraq when a **TERRORIST** group called ISIS took over. After they were gone, wahida returned home and was given a grant by Oxfam to open her own shop. In her district, Sadyia, women were not allowed to go to market or have many freedoms, but with Oxfam's help, wahida is living her life her way and supporting herself. She is considered very brave as she runs her own shop which stays open until midnight!

After an earthquake struck Nepal in 2015, Oxfam helped the recovery work to continue, linking the disaster effort to long-term plans to rebuild.

OXFAM FACT FILE

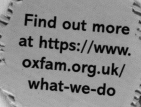

Find out more at https://www.oxfam.org.uk/what-we-do

- **Charity Name:** Oxfam
- **Also Known As:** Oxfam International
- **Started:** 5th October 1942
- **Staff:** Over 5,000
- **Money Raised:** 2015-2016: Over 1 **BILLION** Euros
- **Main Areas:** Poverty, Rights, Emergency Aid and the Right to Be Heard
- **Fundraising:** Donations, Shops, Sponsorship, Festivals & Gifts

PEOPLE & POVERTY

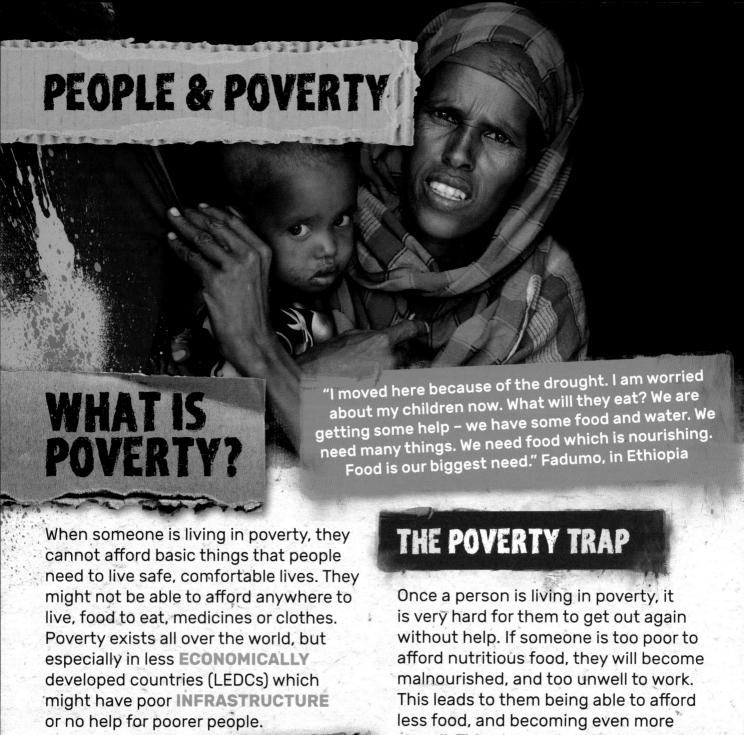

WHAT IS POVERTY?

"I moved here because of the drought. I am worried about my children now. What will they eat? We are getting some help – we have some food and water. We need many things. We need food which is nourishing. Food is our biggest need." Fadumo, in Ethiopia

When someone is living in poverty, they cannot afford basic things that people need to live safe, comfortable lives. They might not be able to afford anywhere to live, food to eat, medicines or clothes. Poverty exists all over the world, but especially in less **ECONOMICALLY** developed countries (LEDCs) which might have poor **INFRASTRUCTURE** or no help for poorer people.

THE POVERTY TRAP

Once a person is living in poverty, it is very hard for them to get out again without help. If someone is too poor to afford nutritious food, they will become malnourished, and too unwell to work. This leads to them being able to afford less food, and becoming even more unwell. This also works with jobs, houses and illnesses. If someone loses their job though illness, they might not be able to afford medicines or look after themselves, and won't be able to get better and look for work. This is called the poverty cycle, or the poverty trap.

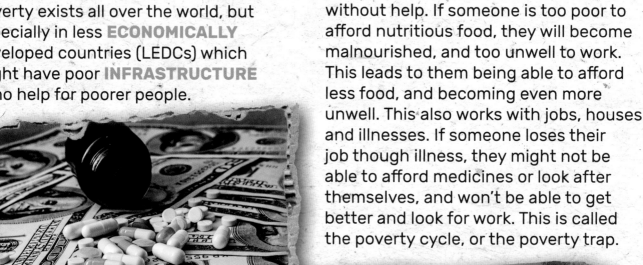

In some countries, medicine is very expensive.

WHAT CAUSES POVERTY?

There are many things that can cause poverty. Here we are going to look at just a few of the main causes.

WAR:

Wars cause people to lose their homes, their jobs and their possessions. This can quickly force people into poverty, and lead to food shortages.

DEBT:

Individual people or whole countries can owe money to others. Countries in lots of debt can end up paying the debts instead of looking after the people.

INEQUALITY:

If a few people have a lot of the money for themselves, it leaves less money for everyone else to share. This creates poverty as there isn't enough to go around.

ECONOMY:

Strong economies make lots of money, and usually mean most people have jobs and can look after themselves. Weak economies mean jobs are lost, which causes poverty.

OVERPOPULATION:

If a country has too many people, it can run out of the resources needed to support them, such as food and houses. These things then become very expensive and people fall into poverty.

EDUCATION:

If people can't educate themselves, they can't get good jobs or learn new skills. A lack of education can be linked to poverty for individual people and whole countries too.

DISASTERS:

Natural disasters, like earthquakes, floods and hurricanes, can destroy people's homes and livelihoods, making them vulnerable to poverty extremely quickly.

WORKING POVERTY

Not everyone who lives in poverty is out of work. Many people who live in poverty have jobs but cannot find enough WORKING HOURS, or their jobs pay such low WAGES that they cannot afford to cover their basic human needs. In turn, it is hard to keep the jobs they have, as they become ill or malnourished and too unwell to work. This can lead to further poverty as they lose jobs or hours.

Elizabeth is 26 and is the mother of two children. She works every day on this rubbish dump in Nairobi, Kenya. She starts at 8am and works through to the evening, but only earns a very small wage. She cannot afford to send her children to school, and sometimes they go and work at the rubbish dump with her instead. Elizabeth has to do this to be able to feed her children, but they still live in poverty.

People who live in poverty face much shorter LIFE EXPECTANCIES and can suffer from mental health problems too.

If children are working and do not get an education, it is very hard to ever get a better job and improve their situations.

GLOBAL POVERTY FACTS

More than three billion people globally live on less than $2.50 per day. That's less than the price of a cheeseburger. More than 1.3 billion of these people live on less than $1.25 per day. This is known as extreme poverty.

One billion children worldwide live in poverty. Children living in poverty or extreme poverty are at risk of dying from illnesses like diarrhoea, pneumonia or cholera. Children in poverty are also at risk of their growth being STUNTED.

More than 750 million people live without access to clean drinking water. This means that they are at risk from diseases carried in the water, and are unable to clean themselves, their clothes or their home.

1.6 billion people live without access to electricity. That is almost a quarter of all human beings. Living without electricity means people have no access to things like washing machines or microwaves, computers or telephones, or even lights in their homes.

Hunger is the number one cause of death in the world. The number of people who die because they can't get enough food is more than the deaths from the three biggest killer diseases – HIV, malaria and tuberculosis – combined.

END EXTREME POVERTY

Oxfam are working in lots of areas around the world to end global poverty and help people to improve their lives.

TIME

One of the most important resources a charity can have is people giving their time. From volunteers working for free to paid, full-time **EMPLOYEES** and celebrity ambassadors, time given to helping people in poverty is vitally important to their work.

VOLUNTEERS

Many people give their time to charities for free, doing things such as collecting clothing and items to sell in the charity shops, or collecting change for donations. Other people might work in a local charity shop or collect money through fundraising. These people are called volunteers.

Oxfam UK works with over 22,000 volunteers, each giving their time to support the charity and its work. Some people give just an hour, and others have volunteered with Oxfam for many years. Some people give their time to promoting campaigns too, or getting people to sign a petition.

From selling clothes in a shop to raising awareness, volunteers are an important part of a charity's work.

EVENT ORGANISER
LOCAL MUSIC, GLOBAL IMPACT

YOUR GIFT IS A TOILET

Here's a gift that has a whole range of benefits. Giving someone access to a composting toilet in a refugee camp or community can save lives by preventing the spread of disease.

Not only that, but it brings dignity to people, and having a toilet in school helps the children to attend

Irene Nzilan and Diana Ayetai from Rueben Baptist Primary school washing their hands in Mukuru informal settlements, Nairobi, Kenya.

Thanks to your gift more people like the students at Rueben Baptist School can have a healthier future.

It's amazing what a decent toilet can do. At Rueben Baptist School in Nairobi, Kenya, enrolment has doubled in the 12 months since they installed Fresh Life toilets.

Previously, the school had unsanitary pit latrines and outbreaks of water-related illnesses were high. But the new Fresh Life toilets have helped create a clean and healthy school environment where the children can study and play.

They also teach children the importance of hand washing, general health and cleanliness. As a result children do not get sick as much and so come to school more regularly.

"I like Fresh Life toilets because they are sanitary, there's tissue, and water for washing your hands."
Pauline Mokaya, student at Rueben Baptist School

See the impact of your gift at
www.oxfamunwrapped.com/yourgift

IN JUST ONE YEAR...

What Oxfam did between 2016 and 2017:

* Responded to 31 emergencies around the world
* Reached 11.6 million people with emergency relief and long-term development
* Inspired 2.3 million people to take action in campaigns
* Worked in over 90 countries

WORKING FOR OXFAM

Many people are so passionate about the fight against poverty that they make it their CAREER. Charities are huge organisations, so there are many opportunities to do something good for a living.

'My name's Shireen and I am Syrian. I have been in Iraq for two years and two months. I work for Oxfam as a public health promoter. I've worked for Oxfam for a year and five months. I sit with people and they are like me; I am a refugee and they are displaced. So we have something we can share. Oxfam did and will do a very good job in Iraq. They are so organized and they care about the most important thing in life, which is water. I would like to ask people from all around the world, in Spain, in England, to support this project because really we are helping people here. We are doing our best and we would like you to support us to do that.'

END EXTREME POVERTY

MONEY

Charities need money to be able to do their work. But where do they get it from?

GIFTS

Wouldn't a goat make a great birthday present? Oxfam raise money by selling virtual gifts. You buy a 'gift' as a present from as little as £5 – anything from a goat to a pile of poo! The money you spend pays for that gift to go to a family who needs it – a goat to give milk, or poo as FERTILISER for a farm. The person you buy the present for gets their name on the gift, and a card telling them where their donation has gone.

Goats give milk, manure and maybe even baby goats! This helps farmers.

DONATIONS

People can give money to Oxfam as a gift. From small amounts of loose change up to hundreds, thousands, or even millions of pounds! Some people give a small amount every month, in a regular payment from their bank account. Even small amounts can add up quickly. You can also donate goods – clothes, books and toys – to an Oxfam shop, where they will be sold to raise money.

Poo, or 'manure', is a great fertiliser for crops.

Find out more at https://www.oxfam.org.uk/shop/oxfam-unwrapped - wouldn't you like a (virtual) pile of poo for your birthday, and to change the world a little bit too?

Fundraising is often done by volunteers.

FUNDRAISING

Oxfam relies on people raising money to support their work. People can raise money in lots of ways – asking lots of people to give just a little, or asking one or two people or big businesses to give a lot!

BUSINESSES & SPONSORS

Big businesses work with Oxfam by donating money, working to raise awareness, or changing the way they work to help animals and wildlife.

These are just some of the brands that support Oxfam's work.

The **co-operative** bank

The Co-Operative Bank

WATERSTONE'S

Waterstones

Innocent

Find out more about how YOU can raise funds for Oxfam on page 26.

Visa Cards

VISA VISA

MARKS & SPENCER

Marks & Spencer

17

END EXTREME POVERTY

AWARENESS

By speaking out to the world about the problems and causes of poverty, Oxfam are able to inspire and MOTIVATE people to support their causes. People are more likely to help if they can see what is happening around the world – it's easy to forget that not everyone's life is like your own.

George* is at hospital here to check his growth and weight. Telling stories like George's helps people understand how and when they can help.

@oxfamgb

@oxfamGB

@oxfamgb

Oxfam GB

SOCIAL MEDIA

Social media is a very powerful tool in raising awareness. Oxfam uses social media to raise awareness, share stories and successes, and let the world know about people living in poverty and how they can help. Ask an adult with an account on one of these sites to show you Oxfam's work, and talk with you about what you see there.

*Names changed to protect the identities of children.

CELEBRITY AMBASSADORS

Many famous people have a lot of fans and followers on social media. This means that they can speak out, and a lot of people will listen. Celebrities working with Oxfam use this opportunity to speak out against poverty, and tell Oxfam's stories.

Celebrity chef, Jack Monroe, has visited Tanzania with Oxfam. You can read more about their experiences at: https://www.oxfam.org.uk/inside-oxfam/jack-monroe-power-of-community

EDUCATION

Oxfam believes in education. Working with schools and teachers to educate and inspire is an important part of their work. Schools can find out more about Oxfam, get involved with fundraising and learn all about poverty and its causes. Oxfam believe young people have a great power to change the future for the better.

Any UK school can book a guest speaker from Oxfam to come to their school. The speakers will tell you and your classmates all about Oxfam and their work, and help you think about what you can do to help bring about change.

Harry Potter actress Bonnie Wright is a big supporter of Oxfam. She travelled to Senegal to raise awareness of issues there. You can read more about Bonnie and Oxfam at https://www.oxfam.org.uk/what-we-do/about-us/ambassadors

Schools can also get actively involved with Oxfam. From raising money to educating ourselves, learning about the world around us – and the world farther away from our daily lives – is important.

We can all learn to make better choices and stand up for what we believe in.

Guest speakers can talk to the whole school in assembly.

Find out how your school can raise money for Oxfam on page 26.

MAKING A DIFFERENCE

Through fundraising, education and awareness, and with the help of staff and volunteers, Oxfam has done some amazing work for people in poverty, changing lives and whole communities all around the world. Here are some stories, showing how the charity has made a difference.

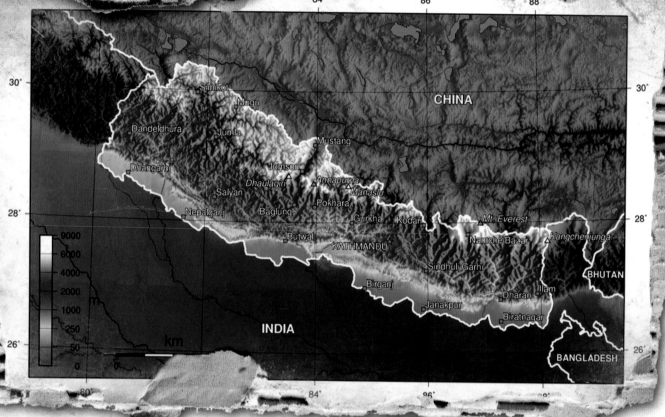

EARTHQUAKE IN NEPAL

On the 25th of April, 2015, a massive earthquake struck Nepal, killing nearly 9,000 people. 850,000 homes were lost or damaged, and many people lost their jobs and sources of INCOME.

Oxfam were already working in Nepal, and were able to respond very quickly. They used stored water to provide drinking water and toilets, and provided thousands of hygiene kits, including toothpaste, shampoo and soap, so people could stay clean. This is very important as it helps prevent illnesses spreading.

Oxfam Hygiene Kit

Families slept on open ground after the earthquake. Oxfam helped to keep them safe.

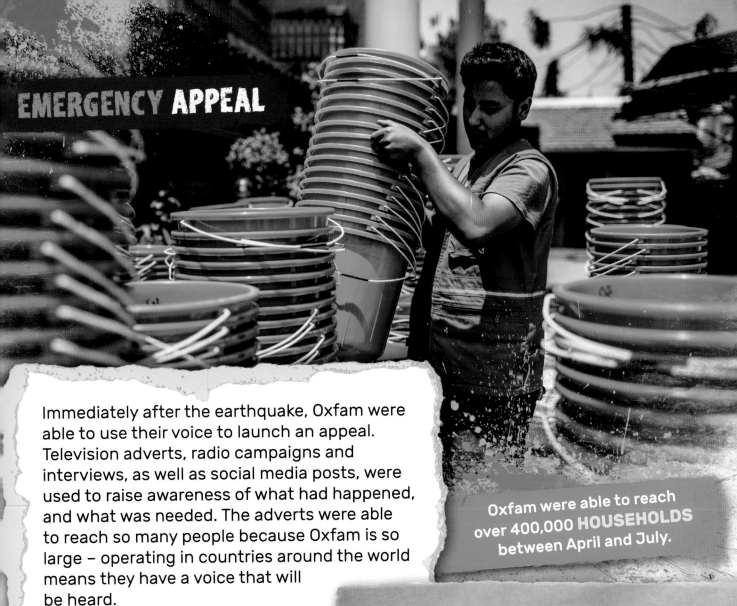

EMERGENCY APPEAL

Immediately after the earthquake, Oxfam were able to use their voice to launch an appeal. Television adverts, radio campaigns and interviews, as well as social media posts, were used to raise awareness of what had happened, and what was needed. The adverts were able to reach so many people because Oxfam is so large – operating in countries around the world means they have a voice that will be heard.

Oxfam were able to reach over 400,000 **HOUSEHOLDS** between April and July.

Even small donations make a big difference.

- £25 provides clean water for four families for a month
- £50 feeds a family for two weeks
- £100 provides emergency shelter for five families

THE LONG HAUL

Planning for disasters and helping people to be better prepared for problems in the future is also very important. Across Nepal, Oxfam had already been working to put disaster measures and emergency plans in place. Oxfam worked with the World Health Organisation, making Tribhuvan University Teaching Hospital in Nepal one of the most earthquake-RESILIENT in the country. The hospital had fully-trained staff, an emergency plan, and earthquake-proof water supplies, and was treating injured people within 20 minutes of the earthquake striking.

Tribhuvan University Teaching Hospital

RESPONDING TO DISASTER

This timeline shows how Oxfam responds to a disaster like the 2015 Nepal earthquake.

Nepal is hit by a huge earthquake

APRIL 25TH, 2015:

1

Hospitals and emergency teams respond immediately

20 MINUTES:

2

Winter shelter kits sent out, including thermal blankets and hot water bottles

OCTOBER 2015:

8

Drinking water systems in operation

SEPTEMBER 2015:

7

Cash For Work schemes begin rebuilding services

NOVEMBER 2015:

9

Training given so people can learn to rebuild

JAN 2016:

10

Camps set up and water provided

APRIL 26TH:

3

Relief goods arrive from Europe and India, including shelters and food

MAY 2015:

4

Vouchers given out to help people buy tools

JULY 2015:

6

Seed bags and agriculture kits sent to help rebuild farms

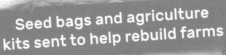

JUNE 2015:

5

Livestock distributed to farms again

MARCH 2016:

11

Rebuilding and recovery in full swing

APRIL 2016:

12

SEND MY FRIEND TO SCHOOL

You and your schoolfriends have the power to do something really important. Not all children around the world are lucky enough to go to school and get an education. As many as 263 million children miss out on regular school, and lack of education traps them in poverty. Oxfam are taking part in the Send My Friend to School campaign. This campaign gives you the power to change that.

Over 10,000 schools and youth groups and millions of children have taken part in the Send My Friend to School campaign.

Send My Friend to School is a national campaign in the UK to help children lucky enough to have access to free, safe education to speak up for children in other countries who don't. Send My Friend to School is a coalition – a partnership of many leading charities and groups, including Oxfam. Coalitions can be very powerful as they join several big voices and use them all to fight one campaign – they can be a very effective way of raising awareness.

FIGHTING FOR AN EDUCATION

MAJID'S STORY

Majid was 15 years old when a terrorist group called ISIS took over the area where he lived. His school was closed, and there was a lot of fighting. Majid and his brother left their home and walked to a refugee camp. Majid had missed two years of school and had to catch up. Now he is studying hard, and hopes to be an Arabic teacher to support his family.

AMNAH'S STORY

Amnah lives in Gaza, an area which frequently experiences violence. Amnah is 12, and loves to read – especially to her little sister, Malak. Amnah often feels scared on her way to school, as she sees soldiers and hears shooting. Sometimes the soldiers threaten her. Amnah and Malak get up very early, so they can walk to school – this takes over an hour. Amnah wants to be a doctor one day so she can treat people and help them.

Bombed Housing Block in Gaza

HOW TO GET INVOLVED

Ask your teacher to check out **www.sendmyfriend.org** and download a pack for your school. The pack will give your teacher lots of resources to help talk about what going to school in other countries is like. It will also help you and your friends from school to speak out and raise awareness.

You can also write letters to:

- Your local politicians
- Local and national newspapers
- The Prime Minister

When we are lucky, it is important that we use our voices to **DEFEND** people who aren't as lucky as we are.

GET INVOLVED

Maybe what you've found out about Oxfam and world poverty has inspired you to take action. Let's look at how you can make a difference and support Oxfam and its work.

DO!

Could you or your school organise a fundraising event? How can you help people living in poverty? Here are some ideas.

SPONSOR ME!

Hold an event, take on a challenge, or do something amazing, and get people to sponsor you. Run, walk, climb, bounce, skip... it's up to you!

SELL, SELL, SELL!

Hold a book sale – maybe you could all donate used books and sell them to raise money for Send My Friend to School? Make sure you tell your customers all about the campaign and why you are raising money.

VOLUNTEER

Is there a local organisation that helps people living in poverty in your local area? Perhaps a responsible grown-up could take you to help?

Stay Safe. Make sure an adult helps you organise your event or goes with you to volunteer.

Shelters for people who are homeless rely on volunteers to serve food and clear up.

DISCUSS!

Become a youth activist and raise awareness in your own community. Here are some ways to get people talking.

WRITE A LETTER

Write a letter to your school newsletter, your local newspaper, or even to the national press! Tell people about what you have found out about people living in poverty, and how they can help.

DAILY NEWS

World - Business - Finance - Lifestyle - Travel - Sport - Weather

Est - 1965

Issue: 240104

THE WORLDS BEST SELLING NATIONAL NEWSPAPER

Monday 5th June

First Edition

World leaders meet in London to discuss the global economy.

The day when representatives of country around the world on, England for talks to wide economic crisis, interest rates, currency, ements, debt, commodity sector wealth will be the sion during this auspicious the worlds super powers.

Some critics are claiming that this will do nothing more than create further problems for poorer nations, but supporters of the initiative are quick to point out that, the forecast predicts nothing but a bleak financial future if things are left the way they are now. Heads of government face further criticism from protesters who state that they should get their priorities in order and..... continued on page 2

ate change - Does cling really make a rence or is history repeating itself?

dies carried out by institues ead that recent weather phe- around the globe may be noth- en nature behaving the way it

and he went on to explain that nothing we do today to protect the environment will have any effect on future atmospheric conditions, or to ensure that our children

THE INSIDE STORY

Have scientists made a major breakthrough in the never ending search for a cure?

Read the full story on - Page 3

Can you live without technology, discover how computers have changed our lives.

Find out more on - Page 11

Working hard for a better lifestyle, but is it damaging your longterm health, read what the experts say.

Examine the results - Page 38

START A CONVERSATION

Ask to speak to your class, or even to your whole school assembly, about Oxfam and their work. Tell them why it matters, what you have read, and how they can help.

AN OXFAM SPEAKER

You can request a speaker from Oxfam to come and speak to your class. There is a small cost to having a speaker in, or you can raise money for Oxfam and a speaker will come and talk to your class about Oxfam and the work they do.

Find out more about booking a speaker at www.oxfam.org. uk/education/get-involved/oxfam-school-speakers

DONATE!

Money, time or goods – everyone can contribute something.

Lots of things can be sold in a charity shop.

CHARITY SHOPS

Could you donate your old books, clothes or toys to an Oxfam shop? Could you ask your whole family to look through their things too? Make sure anything you donate is in good condition; clothes must be clean and with no holes, and toys in good working order.

£5 a month will pay for a goat for two families.

REGULAR DONATIONS

Maybe your family could consider donating a small amount of money every month. Even small amounts can make a difference.

£20 a month could pay for 12 toilets in an emergency zone.

WHERE THE MONEY GOES

For every pound you give to Oxfam:
82p goes directly to ending poverty
10p is spent on support costs – wages and ADMINISTRATION
8p is invested in more fundraising

8p

10p

82p

£42 a month can help provide water to three villages.

SMALL CHANGES, BIG IMPACT

Changing the world starts with changing your world. Little choices we make can make a big difference.

FAIR TRADE

Fairtrade Bananas

When you're shopping, it's important to know that the things you buy – like bananas, chocolate and coffee – have been traded fairly. This means that a fair price was paid to the farmer who grew the produce. Fair trade means everyone gets a fair price for their work, and we pay a fair price for the products. Look for the Fair Trade mark on all sorts of products – even clothes and shoes!

SUSTAINABLE SHOPPING

Can you spot the Fairtrade logo on these bars of chocolate?

Next time you need new clothes, books or toys, perhaps you could try your local Oxfam shop first? You know your money is going to a good cause, and who knows what treasures you might find?

OXFAM:

https://www.oxfam.org.uk/

EDUCATION:

https://www.oxfam.org.uk/education

GIFTS:

https://www.oxfam.org.uk/shop

SHOPS:

https://oxfam.org.uk/shop/shopfinder

SEND MY FRIEND TO SCHOOL:

https://www.sendmyfriend.org/

Write to your local MP to tell them about poverty and show you care: https://www.writetothem.com/

GLOSSARY

ADMINISTRATION	OFFICE-BASED WORK INVOLVED IN RUNNING A BIG COMPANY
BILLION	A THOUSAND MILLION
CAREER	A JOB OR OCCUPATION WHICH A PERSON HAS FOR A LONG TIME
COMMUNITIES	A GROUP OF PEOPLE WHO ARE CONNECTED IN SOME WAY; SOCIALLY, LOCALLY OR BY BELIEF
CONFEDERATION	GROUPS OF ORGANISATIONS OR NATIONS WORKING TOGETHER
GLOBAL COMMUNITY	ALL THE PEOPLE AROUND THE WORLD, WHO ARE CONNECTED TOGETHER IN MANY DIFFERENT WAYS
DEFEND	PROTECT
DONATE	TO GIVE TO A CHARITY FOR FREE
ECONOMICALLY	REGARDING THE WAY TRADE AND MONEY IS CONTROLLED AND USED BY A COUNTRY OR REGION
EMPLOYEES	PEOPLE WHO WORK FOR A COMPANY AND ARE PAID WAGES
FAMINE	A GREAT LACK OF FOOD OVER A WIDE AREA
FERTILISER	A NATURAL OR CHEMICAL SUBSTANCE ADDED TO SOIL TO MAKE IT BETTER FOR GROWING PLANTS
HOUSEHOLDS	A GROUP OF PEOPLE WHO ALL LIVE IN THE SAME HOUSE
INCOME	THE MONEY A PERSON RECEIVES TO LIVE ON
INEQUALITY	THE STATE OF THINGS BEING UNEQUAL, IMBALANCED OR UNFAIR
INFRASTRUCTURE	THE BASIC SERVICES, SUCH AS A POWER SUPPLY AND ROADS, THAT A SOCIETY NEEDS IN ORDER TO FUNCTION
INTERNATIONAL	HAVING TO DO WITH MORE THAN ONE COUNTRY OR NATION
LIFE EXPECTANCIES	HOW LONG MEMBERS OF A POPULATION WOULD BE EXPECTED TO LIVE, ON AVERAGE
LIVELIHOODS	THE MEANS A PERSON HAS OF EARNING OR GETTING WHAT THEY NEED TO LIVE
MOTIVATE	TO CAUSE SOMEONE TO MOVE OR ACT BY GIVING INCENTIVES, REWARDS OR INSPIRATION
PETITIONS	A LIST OF SIGNATURES IN SUPPORT OF AN IDEA OR CAMPAIGN
REFUGEES	PEOPLE WHO HAVE BEEN FORCED TO LEAVE THEIR HOME OR COUNTRY IN ORDER TO ESCAPE DANGER
RESILIENT	ABLE TO WITHSTAND OR RECOVER QUICKLY FROM DIFFICULTY OR CRISIS
RESOURCES	THINGS THAT ARE USEFUL OR OF VALUE
STUNTED	WHEN THE NATURAL GROWTH OF SOMETHING HAS BEEN STOPPED OR SLOWED
TERRORIST	A PERSON WHO CAUSES DAMAGE AND DEATH IN ORDER TO INTIMIDATE GOVERNMENTS OR CIVILIANS
WAGES	REGULAR PAYMENTS EARNED FOR WORK OR SERVICES, USUALLY PAID WEEKLY OR MONTHLY
WORKING HOURS	HOURS WHEN A PERSON CAN WORK OR EARN MONEY

INDEX

Photo Credits

OXFAM PHOTO CREDITS
Pg2 [Tommy Trenchard/Oxfam] **Pg4** [Sam Tarling, UK, 2015.] **Pg6** [Bruno Bierrenbach Feder, South Sudan, 2017.] **Pg7** [Tommy Trenchard, unknown, 2017.] **Pg8** [Abbie Trayler-Smith, Ethiopia, 2016.] **Pg9** [Top: Dalia Ahmed/Oxfam, Iraq, 2017. Bottom: Kieran Doherty, Nepal, 2016.] **Pg10** [Tina Hillier, unknown, 2017.] **Pg12** [Oxfam/Sam Tarling, Africa, 2014.] **Pg14** [Sam Tarling, UK, 2015.] **Pg15** [Top: Allan Gichigi/Oxfam, UK, 2017. Bottom: Tommy Trenchard/Oxfam, Iraq, 2016.] **Pg16** [Katie Richardson, UK, 2016.] **Pg17** [Katie Richardson, UK, 2016.] **Pg18** [Bruno Bierrenbach Feder, Nyal, 2017.] **Pg20** [Pablo Tosco, Nepal, 2015.] **Pg21** [Pablo Tosco/Oxfam, Nepal, 2015.] **Pg22&23** [Top R: Kieran Doherty/Oxfam, Nepal, 2016. Mid L-R: Pablo Tosco/Oxfam, Nepal, 2015. Kieran Doherty/Oxfam, Nepal, 2016. Bottom L-R: Kieran Doherty/Oxfam, Nepal, 2016. Kieran Doherty/Oxfam, Nepal, 2016] **Pg24&25** [Top: Send My Friend/Tom McGuire. Bottom: Send My Friend/Mark Bushnell, Malawi. All other images courtesy of Send My Friend to School.] **Pg28** [Top: Sam Tarling, UK, 2015. Middle: Abbie Trayler-Smith/OxfamAUS, Mozambique, 2014. Bottom: Tommy Trenchard, Balukhali Camp, 2017. Tommy Trenchard/Oxfam, Balukhali Camp, 2017.] **Pg29** [Rachel Manns, UK, 2016.]

Front Cover – Muellek Josef. 4 – szefei, wavebreakmedia, Anan Kaewkhammul. 5 – Rawpixel.com, Michaelpuche, DogStarImages. 6 – Anton_Ivanov, marako85, Artush. 7 – Skowronek, Redrose64, . 8 – Sk Hasan Ali, steve estvanik. 10 – By Maksimilian, Mr_Mrs_Marcha. 11 – By HN Works, Puckung, Leremy, bioraven, supanut piyakanont, SoieiiC, Stanii777. 12 – Yavuz Sariyildiz, 13 – NickKnight, NavinTar, Oxford Media Library, Zvonimir Atletic, Gabbe, mezzotint. 16 – Budimir Jevtic, Eric Isselee. 17 – SpeedKingz, Cristina Nixau, patat, DenisMArt, Valeri Potapova. 19 – Featureflash Photo Agency, Katy Spichal, Jandrie Lombard. 20 – Oxfam East Africa, ElectionworDutourdumonde Photography 21 – Krish Dulal. 22&23 – Oxy_gen, think4photop, RedKoala, VoodooDot, Farah Sadikhova, Mihai Speteanu, Zzvet. 25 – Ryan Rodrick Beiler. 26 – Jacek Chabraszewski, Yulia Grigoryeva, Monkey Business Images. 27 – RTimages, ESB Professional, Rawpixel.com. 28 – Nick Fox. 29 – Thinglass, Jane Rix, Lenscap Photography. Background on all pages: Flas100. Cardboard & Paper – Andrey_Kuzmin, Palokha Tetiana, NLshop, Picsfive, Andrey Eremin, Adam Cegledi, Flas100. ANATOL, Prostock-studio, Elena Polovinko. Images are courtesy of Shutterstock.com. With thanks to Getty Images, Thinkstock Photo and iStockphoto.